BLUE BANNER BIOGRAPHY

Mike
TROUT

Tammy Gagne

Mitchell Lane
PUBLISHERS

P.O. Box 196
Hockessin, Delaware 19707
Visit us on the web: www.mitchelllane.com
Comments? Email us: mitchelllane@mitchelllane.com

Mitchell Lane
PUBLISHERS

Printing   1   2   3   4   5   6   7   8   9

Blue Banner Biographies

Library of Congress Cataloging-in-Publication Data applied for.
Gagne, Tammy.
  Mike Trout / by Tammy Gagne.
      pages cm. — (Blue banner biographies)
  Includes bibliographical references and index.
  ISBN 978-1-61228-466-8 (library bound : alk. paper)
  1. Trout, Mike, 1991– —Juvenile literature. 2. Baseball players—United States—Biography—Juvenile literature. I. Trout, Mike, 1991– II. Title.
  GV865.T73G34 2014
  796.357092—dc23
  [B]
                                                                    2013023040
eBook ISBN: 9781612285238

ABOUT THE AUTHOR: Tammy Gagne is the author of numerous books for adults and children, including Roy Halladay and Buster Posey for Mitchell Lane Publishers. She resides in northern New England with her husband and son. One of her favorite pastimes is visiting schools to speak to kids about the writing process.

PUBLISHER'S NOTE: The following story has been thoroughly researched, and to the best of our knowledge represents a true story. While every possible effort has been made to ensure accuracy, the publisher will not assume liability for damages caused by inaccuracies in the data and makes no warranty on the accuracy of the information contained herein. This story has not been authorized or endorsed by Mike Trout.

PLB

Blue Banner Biography

On September 30, 2012, Angels center fielder Mike Trout made history. He became the first-ever rookie player in the major leagues to hit 30 home runs and steal 40 bases in a single season.

Born to Play Baseball

When Mike Trout blasted a home run against the Texas Rangers on September 30, 2012, he made Major League Baseball (MLB) history. Mike, the centerfielder for the Los Angeles Angels of Anaheim, became the first-ever rookie with 30 home runs and 40 stolen bases in a single season. He barely missed the opportunity to become only the third player to record 30 homers and 50 stolen bases, finishing with 49 steals.

Sportscasters and fans alike had been talking about Mike for some time before he entered the record book. He had already gained a reputation as a powerful, well-rounded player. Boston Red Sox pitcher Clay Buchholz, who had yielded a 445-foot (136 meters) homer to Mike a few weeks earlier, spoke highly of his opponent. He told the *Tribune Business News*, "They call him The Natural on TV, and that's the closest thing that I can say. He can run, he can throw, he can hit, hit for power, hit for average. It's fun to watch him play, just not when you're pitching to him."

Mike Trout comes by his baseball talent naturally. His father, Jeff Trout, was good enough to be taken by the

Minnesota Twins in the fifth round of the 1983 Major League Baseball Draft after being named an All-American his senior year in college. He played four seasons in the minor leagues before a knee injury ruled out playing in the majors one day. Jeff returned to his hometown of Millville, New Jersey, and decided to teach history and coach baseball and football.

He and his wife Debbie—also a teacher—have three children. The youngest one joined the family on August 7, 1991. Not surprisingly, Michael Nelson Trout arrived with the greatest speed. The couple arrived at Newcomb Hospital in the neighboring city of Vineland at four in the morning. Mike was born just three hours later. "He was always fast," his father joked in the *Orange County Register.*

Baseball seemed to be Mike's passion from the time he could walk. "He was always around the field, players and practices," his father told the *Register.* "He'd run around the bases after games and want to be in the action." His parents signed him up for T-ball when he was five. Little League soon followed. "He was so excited before the opening day of Little League that he'd sleep in his uniform," Jeff said. "He was ready to go."

The little kid who was known for his speed loved to spend time outdoors, except when there was a game on. Even when he was just eight, Mike would sit in front of the television for all nine innings. As Jeff pointed out, "Most

> *Baseball seemed to be Mike's passion from the time he could walk. "He was always around the field, players and practices," his father told the Register.*

kids couldn't do anything that long, but Mike was glued to the TV."

Craig Atkinson, one of the family's neighbors, remembers that five-year-old Mike would toss rocks into the air and hit them with his aluminum bat for hours at a time. Millville mayor Tim Shannon, a friend of Atkinson's, told *New Jersey Monthly*, "Craig and I saw him play in an all-star game where he was the littlest kid on the field, and he hit a home run. And we sort of looked at each other, shook our heads and said, 'Whew.'"

Shannon added that "He hit this monster, I mean monster home run out of Folsom, which had a Little League field with a 10-foot-high (3 meters) fence and pine trees. And behind the woods was a cemetery. That's where the ball ended up."

> Mike's father told the South Jersey Times, "It's every athlete's dream to be on the cover of Sports Illustrated. We are proud of him and humbled by it."

That impressive Little Leaguer is now a big leaguer who appeared on the cover of *Sports Illustrated* magazine's August 27, 2012 issue. The caption went one stage beyond Clay Buchholz, calling Mike "The Supernatural" and asking "How Can Mike Trout Be So Good So Young?" When the issue hit the stands, Mike's father told the *South Jersey Times*, "It's every athlete's dream to be on the cover of *Sports Illustrated*. We are proud of him and humbled by it. It's a tremendous thing for a kid from Millville and Cumberland County to be on the cover of *Sports Illustrated*. It's the premier sports magazine in the country."

In the off-season Mike lives with his parents in Millville. No matter how famous he may be, Mike's mother still makes him take out the trash. She told *New Jersey Monthly*, "I'm surprised at how big his success has been so far. But Mike has always had a ball in his hands—a baseball, basketball or football—and was always walking around with it."

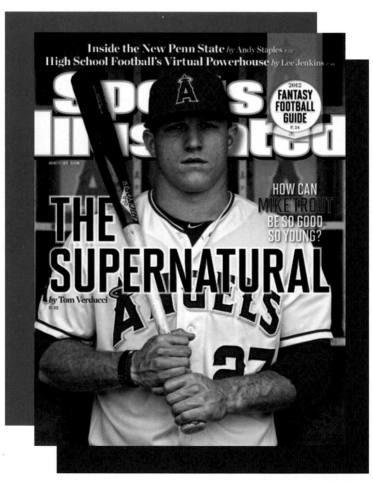

In his story about Mike, writer Tom Verducci said, "By at least one gauge . . . his 2012 performance is the greatest in history by a player age 21 or younger."

A Well-Rounded Player— and Person

By the time Mike was a senior in high school, he was making a name for himself in baseball. Mike was a capable athlete in other sports as well. In basketball he played power forward. On the football team, he played both quarterback and safety. His baseball coaches could put him anywhere on the field. "I was a shortstop until they moved me to the outfield because they thought I was fast," Mike explained to the *Orange County Register*. He also pitched. At this time, though, he wasn't focusing on a future career. "I just liked playing, having fun," he said.

As teachers, Jeff and Debbie raised Mike to put school first. Jeff has said that one of his proudest moments was when Mike made the National Honor Society. He and his wife are proud of their son's success in school and the fact that he is such a respectful and humble young man.

Mike's older sister, Teal, is married with two kids. His older brother, Tyler, is pursuing a law career. Mike told Yahoo Sports that he tips his cap to his big brother. "I wasn't really a school guy. I mean, I got good grades, but it wasn't my thing. I wanted to be outside. He was always studying. . . . It's hard work every day. All this stuff is going to pay off for him."

As humble as he is, though, Mike has always believed in himself. Whether playing baseball or trying something new, he sets goals and goes all-out to meet them. Tyler shared an example with the *Daily Journal*. "He has so much confidence in everything," he said. "He's been begging me to take him crabbing. I'm like, 'Alright, this is going to be terrible. I'll catch like two or three, be bit up by bugs and I'll hate it.' He's like, 'I'm going to catch two or three dozen.' And he does. He knows that's what he's going to do, and he does it."

> "Mikey used to beat us all the time. He'd get up and we wouldn't even try to get him out. He was always the best hitter, and always the fastest," Teal said.

Mike's sister Teal played softball in high school and remembers playing wiffleball with her younger siblings. "Sometimes home plate was my dad's jacket, sometimes it was a paper plate, sometimes my mom's flip-flop was second base," she recalled in the *Daily Journal*. "Mikey used to beat us all the time. He'd get up and we wouldn't even try to get him out. He was always the best hitter, and always the fastest."

Mike has always been known for his positive attitude. Sportswriters have joked that behind Mike's smile is another smile. "He still smiles all the time. I don't think he has ever had a bad day in his life," Jeff told the *Orange County Register*. Mike's favorite movie is the Adam Sandler

Mike has an incredibly positive attitude. Unlike most people he never seems to have a bad day. If he does, he certainly doesn't show it. Family, friends, and even sportswriters can't help but notice that Mike always seems to be smiling.

golf comedy, *Happy Gilmore*. He says he often goes to sleep at night with the movie playing in the background.

Despite his success on the ballfield and all the money it has earned him, Mike lives a very quiet life. He doesn't drink or chew tobacco, a popular but dangerous pastime among baseball players. His taste in music is a bit mellow. He enjoys listening to country artists like Luke Bryan and Brad Paisley.

"My parents are my inspiration. My father who played baseball is my inspiration," Mike told the Orange County Register.

Today Mike sees Jeff and Debbie as his biggest role models. "My parents are my inspiration. My father who played baseball is my inspiration," he told the *Orange County Register*.

His father thinks that Mike has become quite an inspiration himself. Jeff told the *Philadelphia Inquirer*, "He has always been a good role model and teammate, and he is still friends with all the kids he grew up with." Millville is one place where Mike can just be himself. Jeff admits that things are a bit different now. "We're bombarded with requests for signed balls and magazine covers, so that is different. But the town of Millville has been great. They get it. He can still go to his favorite eating places. It's nothing out of control. It's fun. This town has always supported him."

Getting Noticed

Many people in Millville knew who Mike Trout was long before he got to high school. Those who didn't, got to know him when he started making headlines as a member of the Millville High School Thunderbolts. The team hadn't beaten the Vineland Fighting Clan since Mike was playing Little League. When he pitched in a game against Vineland, however, Mike brought home his team's first win against their biggest rival since 2003. Just a sophomore at the time, he pitched the entire game, allowing just two hits. The final score was 2 to 1.

As a junior, he pitched a no-hitter against the Egg Harbor Township Eagles. The Thunderbolts made it all the way to the state playoffs that year. In the end the Cherry Hill East Cougars edged out Millville. It seemed that Mike had developed a reputation as a hitter as well as a pitcher. The Eagles intentionally walked Mike every time he came up to bat. The first time the bases were loaded, and the second time Mike could have won the game if he'd hit a home run.

His talent wasn't going unnoticed outside of Millville either. Scouts from all over the country were coming to Mike's games throughout his junior and senior years. One was Greg Morhardt, who was keeping an eye on Mike for the Los Angeles Angels of Anaheim. Morhardt had played minor league ball with Jeff. He made no secret that he was hoping to sign Mike. He told Mike's father that the high schooler was the best position player prospect he had ever seen.

Morhardt told the *Orange County Register*, "I'll put him against anybody. Sometimes you have to jump out there a little bit. I didn't think there was a better amateur player in the country. At some point he's going to have a chance to be a Hall of Fame baseball player. . . . There are a lot of kids that are strong, and a lot that are fast, but most kids don't have that combination. It's very rare."

Scouts would watch Mike while he was taking batting practice before his games began. Many high school players would have let the pressure of all this attention interfere with their performances. It never distracted Mike from his goals, however. He knew what he wanted, and he was making it happen. "It's a good feeling to have people watch you, and it makes you play better and the team play better," Mike told the *Tribune Business News*.

Mike batted .531 his senior year. He set a South Jersey record by hitting 18 home runs in a single season. He also had 45 runs batted in (RBIs) and helped his team set a school record of 22 wins with just 4 losses. He was named the *Philadelphia Inquirer's* South Jersey player of the year. Mike ended his high school career with a batting average of .461, 31 home runs, and 121 RBIs.

When the time came, Mike became the 25th overall pick in the 2009 draft. The Angels gave him a $1.2 million signing bonus. Mike would be heading west to play in the rookie-level Arizona League.

San Francisco Giants scouting director John Barr regrets his decision to pass over Mike when he made the sixth pick in the draft that year. "He definitely moved a lot quicker and turned out to be a [better] ballplayer a lot quicker than people were anticipating. I think we all look back now and think, 'Geez, we wish he was higher on our boards.'"

Clearly, Millville would miss their star player. When people spoke of Mike, though, it wasn't just his talent that they mentioned. "As good a player as he is, Mike is even a better person," assistant coach Ken Williams told the *Tribune Business News.*

Coach Roy Hallenbeck told the *Philadelphia Inquirer,* "The best thing about Mike is that he never big-leagued anybody and acted like one of the guys. He never separated himself from that group, and we will miss him a lot."

> **When the time came, Mike became the 25th overall pick in the 2009 draft. The Angels gave him a $1.2 million signing bonus.**

A common sight in Major League Baseball:
Mike Trout stealing second base.

On the Move

When Mike joined the Angels' club in Arizona, he made it on base six times in his first professional game. He had a batting average of .360 in 29 games. His speed was proving to be a challenge for many opposing infielders. He was so fast that they found it difficult to throw him out on ground balls.

In August, Mike left Arizona to play for the Cedar Rapids Kernels in the Class A Midwest League. Around this time Mike was moved from shortstop to center field. He would spend most of the 2010 season, his second in professional baseball, with the Iowa-based team as well. Playing in 81 games for the Kernels, he had a batting average of .362.

Then he was promoted to the Class A-Advanced Rancho Cucamonga Quakes in California, where he hit .306. His combined average for the 2010 season was .341. He had 47 extra-base hits, 73 walks, and 56 stolen bases. He received the J.G. Taylor Spink Award as the Topps Minor League Player of the Year. Barely 19, he was the youngest player to win this award. It came with $20,000 that he could donate in any way he wished. He chose to give the money to his high school to renovate the baseball field. In turn, the Millville Board of Education voted to rename the field in Mike's honor.

His third season began as he played center field for the Class AA Arkansas Travelers.

When Los Angeles centerfielder Peter Bourjos suffered a hamstring injury on July 8, the Angels called up Mike. He got off to a slow start, with just 6 hits in his first 34 times at bat.

The afternoon of July 24 was a different story. In the top of the eighth inning, the Angels had a 3–2 lead against the Baltimore Orioles. Mike had managed to hit the second double of his career in the previous game. He had also

After hitting his first MLB home run, Mike (third from left) poses with (from left) Zack Hample (the fan who caught the ball), Mike's father Jeff, his mother Debbie, his brother Tyler, and Mike's girlfriend Jessica Cox.

stolen his first base. When he stepped up to the plate this time, the Angels had runners on first and second. Baltimore relief pitcher Mark Worrell threw Mike three balls and one strike. On the fifth pitch, Mike sent the ball 414 feet (126 meters) into the left field seats. It was his first major-league home run.

Mike was pleased, both with his milestone and with the fact that his family was there to share the experience with him. "It was just awesome out there," he told the *Press of Atlantic City*. "It's definitely special. I think it's my parents' first home run they've seen in pro ball that I hit in a game."

It is common for fans who catch baseballs to try to make deals with the players who want them back as mementos. Zack Hample was no stranger to catching balls. He claimed to have collected 5,200 balls from 48 different ballparks since 1990. The ball from Barry Bonds' 724th career homer is part of his collection. By the time he caught Mike's ball, he had even authored a book called *How to Snag Major League Baseballs.*

> *"A shake of the hand and a sincere thank you is more valuable to me than a physical piece of evidence." Mike was happy to honor Hample's request.*

All that Hample wanted from Mike was a handshake. He told the *Press of Atlantic City*, "A shake of the hand and a sincere thank you is more valuable to me than a physical piece of evidence." Mike was happy to honor Hample's request.

The only thing harder than making the majors is staying there. Mike learned this lesson when he was sent back to the minor league on August 1. He responded to this setback by doing what he always had, working hard. His efforts paved the way for his return to the majors less than three weeks later.

Winning the Marathon

*D*espite a few great moments, Mike was struggling to keep his spot with the Angels. His coaches sent him back to the minors on August 1. Yet again, Mike knew what he had to do to get what he wanted. He flourished once more at the AA level, earning himself another opportunity to play in the majors on August 19 and finished the season with the Angels. Overall he played in 40 games and hit .220. He also became the youngest player since Andruw Jones to hit more than one homer in a single game when he hit two against the Seattle Mariners on August 30.

With such highs and lows, Mike's first season in the majors had turned into quite a roller coaster ride. But he had been brought up to look at the big picture. His father always told him that baseball is a marathon, not a sprint.

Mike began the 2012 season with the Salt Lake City Bees of the AAA Pacific Coast League. Mike had spent his off-season preparing for the marathon, and got off to a great start with the Bees as he hit .403 in the team's first 20 games. When the Angels won only six games out of the first 20, it was obvious that they needed some offensive firepower.

They called him up on April 28. Now a new opportunity was before him, and he was more than ready for it.

Like all good marathoners, Mike started off slowly. It took him about 10 days to get going, but once he did, there was no stopping him. He hit .324 in the month of May and .372 in June. He had more home runs and stolen bases than any other player in the league during those two months. Mike helped the Angels to win 32 of their next 50 games. In the first two and half months of the season, Mike had a slugging average of .550.

When experts predicted that Mike would make it into 2012 All-Star Game, he was hopeful but still his humble self.

Mike has a strong talent for stealing bases. In this 2012 game against the Oakland Athletics, he steals second during the first inning as second baseman Jemile Weeks is too late in applying the tag.

"If I get picked, it'd be a great honor. But if I don't get picked, there's always next year," he told the *Orange County Register*. "It's a good personal goal. But I'm here to win. All the individual honors are nice, but that's not as important as helping the team win."

Mike was named to the American League team as a reserve. "It's a dream come true after all the hard work," Mike told the *Los Angeles Times* when he learned that he had been selected. Though the National League crushed the American League 8–0, Mike had one of the American League's six base hits. He also walked and was the only man on his team to be on base more than once.

Mike is presented with the 2012 Jackie Robinson Rookie of the Year Award before a home game on April 13, 2013. Mike holds the plaque as Angels general manager Jerry Dipoto (on the left) and manager Mike Scioscia look on.

The marathon isn't over for Mike. He definitely played a key role in helping the Angels get as far as they did in their 2012 season. In the end, though, the team barely fell short of making the playoffs. They finished their season with a record of 89 wins and 73 losses. It would be the third straight season the team didn't make the post-season, but with Mike on their side, anything seems possible in upcoming seasons.

Mike may have kept his focus on winning games for his team, but other members of the baseball community did not overlook the personal successes he racked up in the 2012 season. The Baseball Writers Association of America made him the American League Rookie of the Year. The decision was unanimous. Mike became the eighth player in history to earn all 28 first-place votes.

Many people also believed that Mike should have been named the American League Most Valuable Player (MVP). But the voters chose Miguel Cabrera of the Detroit Tigers instead, mainly because he was the first Triple Crown winner in 45 years. That means he had the league's highest batting average and more home runs and RBIs than anyone else.

Mike continued his record-setting in the 2013 season. Against the Seattle Mariners on May 21, he became the youngest player in American League history to hit for the cycle. That means he hit a single, a double, a triple, and a home run in the same game. "It was one of those nights," Mike told *USA Today*. "I didn't really think about it until about the eighth inning. And when I got on deck, I started feeling it a little bit. . . . It was in the back of my mind, trying to hit a home run. I just barreled it up and it went out. It feels great." Mike was also elected to the 2013 All-Star Game as a starter.

Many people are still amazed at Mike's success. Brian Hutchings owns On Deck Sports Cards in Vineland, New

Mike and his teammates celebrate his rare accomplishment of hitting for the cycle on May 21, 2013. The team won the game against the Seattle Mariners with a final score of 12 to 0.

Jersey. He started buying and selling Mike's baseball cards back in 2009. He confided to the *Orange County Register*, "Now, I'm just kicking myself because I see the Trout cards I sold for $30 going for $600 online. That could have been my retirement plan. How could I have known he'd be this good?"

Greg Morhardt could have told him. As he told the *Orange County Register* in 2012, "When you have a guy that athletic and strong and who has those instincts, you break the mold of the normal process. Every once in awhile, you run into a guy like Mike. Mike is up there with the greats of all time at this young age."

Mike has always known that anything was possible. And not surprisingly, he hasn't lost his focus or his humble nature in the midst of all the attention he has received. He shared with Yahoo Sports, "My goal now is to win a World Series and be myself. That's the hardest thing in the game for me, to stay within myself and not try to do too much. Stay with the approach that got me here. For me, that's just being out there, having fun, getting on base. Getting an opportunity to play. You can't take it for granted, for sure. Someday—it could be today and it could be 25 years from now— you never know what can happen. There's a lot of crazy things that could happen."

1991	Michael Nelson Trout is born on August 7.
2007	Pitches a two-hitter against Vineland High School, bringing Millville its first win against the team since 2003.
2008	Leads the Millville Thunderbolts to the state playoffs.
2009	Sets a South Jersey record by hitting 18 home runs. Helps the Thunderbolts set a school record of 22-4. Becomes the 25th overall pick in MLB's player draft. The Los Angeles Angels of Anaheim offer him a $1.2 signing bonus. Plays for the Arizona Halos and the Cedar Rapids Kernels.
2010	Gets promoted to the Rancho Cucamonga Quakes.
2011	Gets called up to the majors. Hits his first MLB home run. Gets sent back to the minors, but returns to majors before the end of season.
2012	Becomes youngest rookie ever to hit 30 home runs and steal 40 bases. Plays in the All-Star Game. Appears on the cover of *Sports Illustrated* magazine. Is named the 2012 American League Rookie of the Year. Finishes second in American League Most Valuable Player voting.
2013	Becomes the youngest American League player to hit for the cycle (single, double, triple, and home run in the same game). Is elected to the All-Star Game as a starter.

CAREER STATS

Season	G	AB	R	H	HR	RBIs	S	W	SB	AVG	SLG
2011	40	123	20	27	5	16	30	9	4	.220	.390
2012	139	559	129	182	30	83	139	67	49	.326	.564
Total	179	682	139	209	35	99	169	76	53	.306	.532

G = Games
AB = At Bats
R = Runs
H = Hits
HR = Home Runs
RBIs = Runs Batted In
SO = Strikeouts
W = Walks
SB = Stolen Bases
AVG = Batting Average
SLG = Slugging Percentage

Find Out More

Donovan, Pete, Arte Moreno, Tim Salmon, and Mike Scioscia. *Under the Halo: The Official History of Angels Baseball.* San Francisco, California: Insight Editions, 2012.

Mike Trout Stats, ESPN

http://espn.go.com/mlb/player/stats/_/id/30836/mike-trout

Mike Trout, Los Angeles Angels of Anaheim http://losangeles.angels.mlb.com/team/player.jsp?player_id=545361#gameType='R'&sectionType=career&statType=1&season=2012&level='ALL'.

Works Consulted

_____. "Fan gives Mike Trout first home run ball in exchange for a handshake." *Press of Atlantic City*, July 29, 2011.

_____. "Mike Trout hits for season's first cycle in Angels win." *USA Today*, May 22, 2013.

Brookover, Bob. "Millville's Mike Trout Wins AL Rookie of the Year." *Philadelphia Inquirer*, November 13, 2012.

Brown, Tim. "Mike Trout makes on-the-job training look easy as key cog in Angels' push toward top of AL West." Yahoo Sports, June 13, 2012. http://sports.yahoo.com/news/mike-trout-makes-on-the-job-training-look-easy-as-a-key-cog-in-angels--push-in-al-west.html

Calcaterra, Craig. "Shocker: The Angels Call Up Mike Trout." Hardball Talk, NBC Sports, July 8, 2011. http://hardballtalk.nbcsports.com/2011/07/08/shocker-the-angels-call-up-mike-trout/

Caldwell, David. "Millville Slugger: Mike Trout's Monster Season." *New Jersey Monthly*, January 15, 2013.

Fletcher, Jeff. "Scout's Honor: Greg Morhardt Began Filing Almost Unbelievable Reports on a Prospect in 2008. This Week, Mike Trout is Poised to Win AL Rookie of the Year and is an MVP Contender." *Orange County Register*, November 11, 2012.

HalosHeaven.com, Mike Trout's 25th Home Run, Torii Hunter's Sac Fly, Angels 6-5 over Red Sox http://www.halosheaven.com/2012/8/28/3276071/ whoops-halos-win-halos-win-6-5-over-red-sox

HalosHeaven.com, Trout Firsts: Home Run #1 July 24, 2011 - Camden Yards http://www.halosheaven.com/2012/12/17/3774188/ trout-firsts-home-run-1-july-24-2011-camden-yards

Mike Trout, JockBio.com http://www.jockbio.com/Bios/M_Trout/M_Trout_bio. html

Narducci, Marc. "Millville's Trout is S.J. Baseball Player of the Year." *Tribune Business News*, June 12, 2009.

Peltz, Jim. "Angels rookie Mike Trout is selected to All-Star game." *Los Angeles Times*, July 1, 2012.

Plunkett, Bill. "Trout, Trumbo Can Look to the Stars." *Orange County Register*, June 26, 2012.

Plunkett, Bill. "Trout's Home Run Ball Makes Return Trip to Him." *Orange County Register*, July 25, 2011.

Smith, Marcia C. "Card Sharks Eat Up Trout: The Prices Are Sky-High for Memorabilia of the Reigning AL Rookie of the Year." *Orange County Register*, January 29, 2012.

Smith, Marcia C. "Father's Day gives Trouts Another Reason to Smile." *Orange County Register*, June 16, 2012.

Tomase, John. "Red Sox No Match for Mike Trout." *Tribune Business News*, August 29, 2012.

Verducci, Tom. "Kid Dynamite." *Sports Illustrated*, August 27, 2012.

GLOSSARY

bombard (bom-BAHRD) — Address continually without letup.

draft (DRAFT) — Selecting new players who have not competed professionally.

humble (HUHM-buhl) — Not proud or arrogant; modest.

intentional (in-TEN-shuh-nuhl) — Done on purpose.

memento (muh-MEHN-toh) — An item that serves as a reminder of a past event.

milestone (MIYL-stohn) — A significant event within one's life or career.

on deck (awn DEK) — The batter who will be up next

rookie (RUH-kee) — An athlete playing his or her first season as a member of a professional sports team.

runs batted in (RUHNS BAA-tehd IN) — The number of runs that result from a batter's at-bat; for example, if a batter doubles with the bases loaded and all three runners score, the batter is credited with 3 runs batted in.

scout (SKOUT) — A person whose job is to look for talented young athletes for a particular sports team.

slugging average (SLUH-ging AV-uhr-ij) — The number of total bases a batter achieves divided by the number of times at bat; a player with a single, a double, a triple and a home run in 11 at-bats has 10 total bases for a slugging percentage of .909.

unanimous (yoo-NAN-uh-muhss) — A vote in which there is total agreement as to the outcome.